LEARN to SWIM

GREG!

THANKS FOR
LENDING YOUR
BREWERY FOR
MY WORDS!

Learn to Swim

by Joseph Edwin Haeger

This book published by University of Hell Press.
www.universityofhellpress.com

Book Design by Vince Norris
www.norrisportfolio.com

Published in the United States of America.
ISBN 978-1-938753-16-9

"There is a constant flow of feelings in a person's life"

—Ryan Emery

Year I

"Why did you use your wipers?"

"It's raining," I said.

"What happened to making life art?"

* * *

He hugged me harder than anyone ever had.

* * *

I met him in fifth grade. He had moved from Seattle. We were in the same class. We were on the same soccer team. And we went to the same church.

I walked up to him and asked how he liked playing soccer.

He stared up at me from his desk.

"I don't play soccer," he told me.

I saw him that night at practice.

* * *

We began a casual conversation at soccer games. Nothing that I would have expected to lead to a friendship. I was content with the friends I had and didn't think I needed any more. Talking with him was just something to pass the time.

The coach played the same boys every game, for the entire game. He and I would stand on the sidelines, restless, and eventually get bored and wander away from the sport we were supposed to be playing.

One day we were on a shed. Not for any particular reason; we just realized we were big enough to climb on top of it. It wasn't tall, but seemed like it was at the time.

An Elderly Man walked up to us and said, Hey get off that shed, you two shouldn't be up there.

I've always lived the life of a coward. I began to step down until I noticed him.

He stood tall, looking down at the Elderly Man. He wasn't attempting to get down.

You guys need to get down, the Elderly Man repeated.

I continued my way down.

He stared the man in the eyes.

"No, you bitch."

The conclusion begins its downward slope.

* * *

When he first moved here he sat with the cool kids at lunch. He was becoming one of them in the first two weeks.

He played footsie with the cute girls.

He played tag football at recess with the boys.

Then we started talking and he sat with me and the other self-declared rejects at lunch.

I wonder if he ever regretted this decision.

* * *

When did we grow up?

* * *

He came to stay over one night. It was the first time we were spending the night at one another's house. He had packed a bag with all the necessities.

I used to go to friends' houses in jeans, a T-shirt, and with a toothbrush.

My Cousin was there. We were watching movies and getting rowdy.

My Cousin jumped on his back when he was bent over.

Tears came to his eyes as he packed his bag, preparing his exit.

My Cousin apologized.

He made his way to our front door with his bag in hand.

"How are you going to get home?"

"Walk," he told me.

"It's midnight."

He looked at me. Dropped his bag. And followed me back to the living room.

"Sorry," I said. "We'll calm down."

* * *

I woke up to a phone call.

* * *

He told me he was so near a tornado he saw a floating house.

He told me he was in an earthquake where the earth burst and split open. That His Mom purposely drove the car in front of them into the crack. That His Mom killed a man.

He told me he had a half-brother.

I still don't know if I believe him.

* * *

We lived a fourth of a mile apart. It was the same suburban neighborhood. We would ride our bikes to each other's houses.

Our desires matched more closely than I had originally anticipated.

When we rode in our parents' cars no one could understand what we were saying.

But we understood each other's mumblings.

* * *

In his basement there was a crawl space behind the furnace. It was under the stairs.

We crawled back there with a flashlight.

Girls, from the previous owner, had left the names of the boys they liked scrawled on the drywall.

We also found a crude felt-pen replica of a famous piece of art.

We both decided it was the *Mona Lisa*.

* * *

It's like that Boy Meets World *episode where Cory gets married.*

* * *

Kids from another team stomped on my water bottle and put bits of dirt and grass in it.

Our coach patted me on the shoulder and said, Just wash it out at a sink, good as new.

I watched the kids from the other team run to their rides home.

"I hate our coach," he said, "he's a dumb asshole."

We didn't want to play soccer anymore.

* * *

We sat at the counter waiting for the macaroni and cheese to finish cooking.

My Dad asked him what his family was eating that night.

"Steak."

You're picking this over steak? My Dad asked, Why?

All he did was shrug his shoulders.

I would've rather had macaroni and cheese at that age, too.

* * *

I convinced him to join my music club. If I brought them new members I got five free CDs. He would get seven for joining.

He didn't have money to pay for shipping and handling.

He woke up one morning to His Dad on the phone telling the club's customer service that they couldn't enter into a contract with an eleven-year-old boy.

I never asked him to join another club.

* * *

He liked playing computer games. I never understood why he would pour hours into these virtual worlds.

He tried to get me to play once.

I was content watching him play over his shoulder.

* * *

Our group of friends used to play out court at recess sometimes.

I was always the defending lawyer.

The Blond-Haired Boy was the judge. The Blond-Haired Boy always had a pocket Bible. We would all swear upon it before we started the trial.

Our Redneck Friend was the prosecuting lawyer.

The Leftovers were the jury.

Whoever was the defendant would get banished from playing with us for a certain amount of recesses.

He was banished for a day.

He called me that night to see if he was still banished.

Would Jesus banish someone? My Mom asked.

I called him back.

* * *

He told me years later he didn't know why he was such a dick that day.

"I must've woke up and thought, 'I'm going to be an asshole today.'"

It was a half-day and I went to school excited because of that fact. I arrived to him spitting in my hair. Pushing me over when I went to tie a shoe. Calling me mean names. And I had no idea why.

During recess I snapped and punched him. That was the first time I was angry enough to punch someone.

When he saw the rage on my face he ran. I tackled him and pummeled the back of his head.

I ignored the whistle and shouts from the playground supervisor. I only wanted him to feel pain. I hated him in that moment.

Two days later we were back to understanding each other's mumbles.

* * *

We rented *Can't Hardly Wait*. We watched this movie at least two times a year after that.

No one has ever laughed as hard as us when we watched it together.

It's not as funny when I watch it by myself.

* * *

He got his braces taken off. His teeth still didn't look quite right. A year later they put braces back on.

* * *

Have you seen *Dirty Harry*? His Dad asked.

"No," I replied.

Come on, His Dad said, you're a movie guy, that one is a classic, you need to watch it.

He and I never did watch it.

* * *

They found him in the backseat.

* * *

His parents got an aboveground pool you could fill with a hose.

The water was freezing.

His Dad wouldn't let us swim during the rainstorm. There had been thunder.

We thought it would have been fun.

* * *

I didn't think I needed any more friends.

I didn't think I wanted any more friends.

I was wrong.

Year II

Only in death are you completely free(?)

* * *

In sixth grade he got in a fight with a Tall Boy. He was smaller,

but was able to get in on the inside and punch the Tall Boy in the stomach.

He was soft-spoken most of the time, but there were moments when he would lose control. When he would need to prove his worth.

* * *

We were riding our bikes over to his house.

I had three movies in my right hand, so I was riding only with my left hand.

I needed to slow down, but the brake handle was on the right side.

I didn't know the tire and handles would shift that much.

I cradled my movies to protect them from being broken. I hit the ground rolling and scraped my arms and legs. But the movies were safe.

"Are you okay?" he asked.

"Yeah, I'll be fine."

* * *

We would put on a CD and jump around his room. Pretend to mosh as if we were at the actual concert.

* * *

I got a disposable camera and told him we should take pseudo-senior pictures.

"Why?" he asked.

"We're going to have to do it someday," I responded.

"Sounds like a waste of film."

* * *

I couldn't find the troll.

* * *

He missed the first week of school.

I hadn't talked to him. I began to get worried.

I rode my bike to his house that Saturday.

He told me that a bee stung him just under the eye the day before school. One eye swelled up the first night. The next morning both his eyes were swollen shut.

No one would have expected him to react that way to a little sting.

* * *

I made fun of the way he held the baseball bat. I shouted from center field, laughing at his inexperience. His hands weren't together.

He hit the ball over my head.

* * *

During the worship music he raised his hands in praise. I swayed my weight between my feet.

After the service we stood outside at the drinking fountain.

"It's a lot easier to get into worship here," he said, "at home I always fall away."

* * *

I told him to Google search a pretty girl's name.

He said His Mom had the parental control settings turned on.

* * *

We were snowboarding.

He had the kind of bindings that you stepped into and the boots clicked into place.

We got to the bottom of the hill and decided to go eat.

His right boot was stuck because of ice. He kicked the board to get his foot out. His snowboard slid down a hill into some trees. He had to crawl down into the trees to get it. It was a rental.

He had trouble getting back up.

* * *

"Your brother has really affected me."

"Yeah?"

He smiled and gave me a hug.

"We're all going to die. I know now that we can't waste our time on the shitty aspects."

* * *

I tried hitting a tennis ball off a water tee ball stand. It was built for Wiffle balls. The bouncy rubber weighed close to the cylinder spraying the water.

The plastic shattered when the bat made contact.

"That is my sister's," he said.

I felt bad. And I was nervous to get in trouble.

"It's okay. I'll tell them I did it."

He never told me if they asked him about it or not.

* * *

His Mom made him act in a skit for church. He played a mime.

I don't know if it was the makeup or him, but he looked miserable.

* * *

"I mean, just speaking to someone and explaining your feelings exactly how they are is hard enough."

* * *

We were walking on the trails behind my house, in the thickest part of the trees.

A beehive hung in a tree.

We started throwing rocks at it, trying to knock it down.

We missed every time and the rocks rolled down the hill.

A man shouted up, Whoever is throwing rocks, stop it, you're hitting houses.

We didn't know there were houses down below.

* * *

We made an obstacle course in his backyard. It wasn't difficult. Or fun, for that matter.

But we spent hours on it. Trying to reach new personal records.

* * *

We tried making our own comic books: drawing, writing, designing.

My character was called Stupid Man.

His was Mental Man.

Each issue had the same story with a different villain.

* * *

I threw insult after insult at him one afternoon. I was just messing around, but everything I said was at his expense.

I don't know why I got so angry when he tossed one back.

I told him to get out. Leave. Don't say anything, just get out.

I stood in my room for a moment, cooling off.

I left my room and saw him sitting at our computer desk.

"What are you doing?"

He shrugged.

"Get out," I said.

He stood up and pushed me. I punched him in the stomach. He ran by me as if to make an exit. As soon as I took chase he turned and punched me in the nose. My nose became a fountain.

You don't punch people, My Mom shouted. He left through the front door.

I still don't know why I got so angry.

I know I deserved the bloody nose, though.

* * *

What is the benefit in being omniscient?

* * *

Through the woods behind my house was a bicycle loop. It was a few miles away. It was a course designed for BMX bikers.

There was a starting ramp and six or seven jumps throughout the loop.

I had a BMX bike. He had a mountain bike.

He asked if he could borrow my bike.

"Only if you don't crash."

"I won't," he said. "Just let me."

Normally, it took about two minutes to get back to the starting ramp. I had stood there for five minutes.

I got on his mountain bike and rode the course. Twenty-five percent of the way through I saw his legs sticking out of a bush.

"Are you okay?" My bike was laying on his chest.

He moaned.

He took the ramp too fast at an awkward angle.

* * *

The Boy with Red Hair wasn't letting us into the house. When we asked why, the Boy with Red Hair wouldn't give us a reason.

Leaving the door open the Boy with Red Hair went to answer the phone.

He and I snuck into the kitchen and found Pop-Tarts in the toaster. We popped them up and took them with us to our bikes. The Boy with Red Hair was still in the bathroom when we left.

* * *

He said his nose was big because he broke it.

He tried to go off a big bike jump back in Colorado. Once airborne he drifted backwards into the makings of a back flip.

He said he didn't make it all the way around.

* * *

I had my hair bleached blond a lot of the time in grade school. It was because My Mom was a hairdresser and didn't care what I did with my mop top. He decided to do it once, too. People called him Glowworm the next day. After school he was back at my house asking My Mom to dye it back to the normal brown.

My Mom asked if My Brother got made fun of for having dyed hair.

My Brother said yes.

"What did you do when they said stuff?" he asked.

I told them to blow it out their ass, My Brother said.

He decided to keep the blond hair.

That night at church we were talking when a girl looked over at him.

The girl smiled, Hey, you dyed your hair.

He looked embarrassed. Then angry.

"Go blow it out your ass!"

The girl turned red and walked away.

"Dude, she wasn't making fun of you."

* * *

We were at his lake cabin for the weekend.

His Dad told me we were going to snipe hunt one night. I didn't know what a snipe was. His Dad told me, A bird with sharp, fatal claws and three eyes; one on the back of its head.

They had me rub raw, dead fish all over my body. The smell was supposed to attract the rare bird.

He ran through the brush making a lot of noise. I sat on a bench with a baseball bat, terrified.

"It'd be cool if they were real," I said to him, after learning of the hoax.

* * *

He let me borrow his astronomy book for class.

* * *

The next day I didn't have to go to school.

My Grandfather and I weren't particularly close like My Grandfather and My Brother were.

I waited for school to end. He came over and we stood outside. I was trying to balance on a curb.

He asked me if I was sad. I said no. I don't know why, but none of it seemed real. Or it seemed too real.

The routine of life: Get born—grow up—get old—die.

Year III

It rained all three days we were there.

* * *

He threw the bat after he struck out.

Our coach yelled at him, You don't ever, ever throw a bat.

* * *

Force Trauma to the Chest.

* * *

The Boy with Red Hair, the Funny Boy, and he got arrested and taken to juvie.

It was raining so they went into a house under construction.

They were making new additions to our neighborhood. There had been reports of vandalism.

A Cop told them to come out over an intercom.

The three boys tried to sneak out through a basement window.

The Cop tackled the Funny Boy and yelled at the others to come out on their stomachs. They were in seventh grade.

They were given used, purple underwear after being strip-searched.

"The guards joked about Courtney Love all night," he said. "It kept me up."

* * *

I let him borrow one of my fantasy books.

The next time I saw it the cover had been ripped off.

"What the hell, dude?" I asked.

"Sorry, it was in my backpack."

I took the book back as he tried to tell me the library could fix it. He claimed he was going to take it there that afternoon. I put the book in my backpack. He didn't finish reading the novel.

I didn't even like fantasy a year later.

* * *

I got a drum set. He got a guitar. Our Friend with Glasses got a bass. None of us knew how to play.

During our first official band practice he played guitar with his thumbs.

We all thought the riff sounded cool.

* * *

We were both on the line between lightweight and heavyweight.

At first we thought we would do better on the bigger football team so we drank protein shake after protein shake. We were trying to gain five pounds.

His Dad came in and asked why we wanted to be the small guys on the team. We hadn't thought about it that way.

So we spent three days running around our neighborhood trying to lose five pounds.

On the day of weigh-ins he was at one hundred and twenty-two pounds. I was at one hundred and twenty-five.

The cut off was one hundred and twenty-five.

They let me be on the lightweight team.

* * *

In math class we would ignore the busywork and focus on drawing fake movie posters.

We had so many ideas.

* * *

We went back to our elementary school because his sisters had science fair projects.

There was a Fat Boy a year younger than us that started pushing me.

I told the Fat Boy that I didn't want to fight. The Fat Boy continued to push me so I pushed back. The Fat Boy jumped on me, knocking both of us over. We rolled around in the grass in a pathetic attempt at fighting. I punched the fat stomach and my hand was lost in the flesh and fabric.

He ran up and kicked the Fat Boy in the ribs, freeing my hand and body.

He helped me up and we looked at the Fat Boy clutching, writhing in pain.

He didn't say anything. We just walked away.

* * *

We didn't have all the same classes. Only two. And different lunches.

We hung out after school.

* * *

We were in math class one day. The past three months' worth of notes were due.

When he stood up to turn them in Our Friend with Long Hair pulled the notes out of his hand and ripped them in half.

"Fuck!" he screamed.

Our teacher looked over and said, Hey guys, if you curse, just try to curse quietly, please.

I don't know why Our Friend with Long Hair ripped his notes in half. He took Scotch Tape and did his best to put the two halves back together. I thought it looked okay.

Our teacher wouldn't accept his notes.

It dropped his final grade a letter.

* * *

"If you drive fast enough you can't feel the potholes."

* * *

I don't know why I started on drums and him on guitar.

We were always better at each other's instruments.

* * *

Our Friend with Long Hair thought it would be funny to make fifty different laughs. And then laugh all of them.

"That's not funny," he said.

* * *

My Brother had some kind of penis fungus. I don't know for sure if it was sexual or not, but I don't think My Brother was having sex at that point.

My Brother started calling me a faggot one morning and ended the torture by jumping on my bed, naked. My Brother rolled around, laughing at my horror.

"Fuck you," I said. "I'm telling mom."

I walked away but My Brother jumped up and grabbed me. My Brother threw me on the ground and started punching me in the chest. Hard.

You're going to tell Mom, you little faggot? My Brother yelled in my face, Are you still going to?

"Yes."

My Brother continued to beat me in the chest. I began to cry. Fuck you, you fucking baby faggot! My Brother screamed.

My Brother ran to the kitchen and grabbed a knife. If you tell mom I'm going to fucking kill myself. Are you going to tell her?

I got up and went to get my bike. I heard the bathroom door slam.

I rode over to his house. He came out. I was crying.

"Do you want to go find your mom?" he asked.

I nodded.

We found her at the river.

By the time we got home My Brother had gotten bored and ridden to a friend's house.

* * *

Sometimes I would see him at school wearing purple sweatpants.

He would get in trouble for wearing his jeans too low.

* * *

Build a spider web.

Is it fate that decides whether the web causes love or death? Peace or war? Happiness or sadness?

It makes me wonder: How far back can cause and effect go.

* * *

I started calling him Gomer Pyle as a nickname. I don't remember why. He took it as an insult and tried to rename me Stubs.

His nickname stuck for two years.

Mine didn't last two hours.

* * *

We made a short video where I shot him in the leg with a plastic assault rifle.

The final frame of the video was him giving the thumbs up and looking into the camera, saying, "I'm okay."

"Do I have to say 'I'm okay?'" he asked.

"Yes."

"Why?"

I didn't want to get in trouble for shooting my friend in a video.

"It makes it stupid," he said.

"No it doesn't. What if my mom sees it?"

"So what? Tell her that you made a movie," he said. "Don't make it stupid."

* * *

He got Sublime's *Greatest Hits*.

"Where did you get this?"

"Fred Meyer."

"Where'd you get the money?"

He told me that our Friend with Gangly Arms stole it for him.

They would cut the plastic with a razor blade and slip the disc out, putting an empty case back on the shelves. They asked me if I wanted them to get any CDs for me. I said "no."

It didn't feel right to me.

* * *

A girl from school was throwing an end of the year party.

He was invited along with a few other friends.

I didn't get an invitation.

The girl that I liked at the time told me I could come, You don't need an invitation.

I still didn't feel right about it so I decided to play baseball instead.

He was running to the car when he asked if I was sure about not going.

"Yeah," I said. "Have fun."

"Alright, I'll see you later."

* * *

We starting trying to play cover songs.

Sometimes we would try to write our own songs.

We never did write a full song at that age.

* * *

I told him once that he reminded me of My Brother.

"Why?"

"I don't know," I said, "you wear a hat all the time."

"That's why you say I'm like your brother?"

"I guess so."

"I'm not like your brother."

Now that I think about it, I think it was his attitude towards life.

He wasn't afraid of it.

* * *

We were at the mall one day and I pointed at a sweatshirt.

"That's the sweatshirt I'm going to ask my mom for."

"That's pretty cool," he said.

He didn't seem overly interested. I thought it would be a nice addition to my wardrobe.

A week later he came to school wearing the same sweatshirt.

* * *

Sometimes I felt like he had a new best friend.

He always talked about what he did with his Friend with a Face Mole. They would do things during school and after school. Even on the weekends. Going to the mall and riding bikes to where they could take them off jumps. I was jealous that I didn't have a new best friend, too.

I was wrong, though.

Whenever I asked him to hang out he was always there.

If I ever needed anything he was there.

Year IV

Who knew God could be so malignant.

* * *

We swam out to the nearest buoy.

It didn't look to be that much of a swim. We were wrong.

Fire burned in my lungs. I held on to the floating object afraid of the future. Neither of us wanted to swim back.

I was still trying to catch my breath when he said he was going back to the shore.

"Wait for me," I said.

But he had already started swimming.

* * *

He got a white sweater from one of the more popular stores.

I called it his preppy sweater. If he wore it and I was around he would get called preppy by not only me, but any other boy that was around.

I think he only wore it once or twice after that.

* * *

I made the varsity football team. He was on junior varsity.

He continued to become better friends with his Friend with a Face Mole.

I started making more friends.

He and I still hung out every weekend.

* * *

In the summer we would swing from tree branches.

In the winter we would take sleds off jumps.

We tried making extreme videos. They were never very extreme.

Except when he would go.

He always managed to land on his head.

* * *

His Mom paid us in advance to dig up two shrubs in their front yard.

It was hard work.

We only did one. We gave half the money back.

* * *

We were in the pool swimming. We had only been in for about twenty minutes when two girls came to the poolside.

The Girl with a Nice Smile liked him, a lot.

The Girl with a Nice Smile wanted to impress him by jumping into the water fully clothed.

We watched the action. Then silence arose from the pool.

"You want to go back to the room?" I asked him.

"Sure."

* * *

I woke up to a scream.

* * *

Frontline was a church trip to Denver. I decided to go the day before we left. I didn't like leaving home. He was going and wanted me to go as well.

I got homesick after two days.

* * *

During the summer we tried to learn to skateboard. We stood in the middle of the street with our boards looking like a couple of punks.

By the end of the season I could only land a heel flip half the time.

But whenever he tried any trick he would kick the skateboard five feet away from him.

I'm surprised he could stand on the board without falling.

* * *

Our Alcoholic Science Teacher made me read two paragraphs instead of the usual one from the textbook.

It took me a year to realize why.

He sat there with muffled laughter. I didn't know why.

The word "organism" was riddled throughout the two paragraphs.

I wonder if people thought I did it on purpose.

* * *

The tire on my bike went flat.

He told me the way to find the hole was to pull the tube out, fill it with air and then stick it in a bucket of water. When air bubbles filled the bucket you could find the hole.

The self-patching kit only cost five dollars.

We spent an afternoon looking for the holes.

It was easier said than done.

* * *

At his lake cabin we would swim thirty feet from the shore.
There were big rocks under the surface.

On top of these rocks we looked like we were standing on the
water.

* * *

Our Friend with Red Hair and he went down to the Oregon
Coast for a weekend. When he got back he told me about his
second night there.

They were walking on the beach and heard the noise of a party
drifting over a hill. Instead of going over and joining the people
at the bonfire they dropped to their stomachs and crawled up a

– 58 –

dune, just enough to peek over.

This was the first time he saw a real live naked breast. All the girls had their tops off; some were swimming, others just hanging out and talking.

That night he was laying in his sleeping bag when he heard our Friend with Red Hair moan. The sound of rubbing sped up and slowed down.

"Did you tell him to stop?"

"No," he said. "I didn't want to make it any more awkward."

He had pretended to be asleep until he actually was.

* * *

We both wanted to get six-pack abs.

I had an awkwardly shaped body in my adolescence.

He got close, but never quite made it all the way.

* * *

Our first rock concert was the Red Hot Chili Peppers and Stone
Temple Pilots. My Sister drove us and chaperoned.

After STP played their opening song the arena security came
and pulled My Sister into the lobby. My Sister didn't return until
STP had finished their set. That was the band My Sister really
wanted to watch.

Some people had their car broken into and their tickets were
stolen. They didn't remember what their seats were so they made
some up to give to security.

They happened to be our seats. But we didn't steal anything.

* * *

We both tried out for baseball. He was put on the junior varsity
team. I was a floater, meaning I went between varsity and junior
varsity.

I liked playing the junior varsity games more. It was more laid-back.

The varsity team took things too seriously.

* * *

The girl I liked happened to like him. So they started dating.

My chest hurt every time I saw them hug or smile at one another.

One day when I saw them hug, he and I made eye contact. All I could do was stand up and walk away. I didn't want to look at them anymore.

He broke up with her the next day.

"I knew you liked her."

"I know."

"I'm sorry," he said.

"Thanks."

* * *

My Brother got a car.

He and I asked for a ride to school one morning.

Eazy-E blared when My Brother dropped us off.

That was the only time we ever got a ride.

* * *

I tried lighting numerous firecrackers at once. I had them stacked and lined on a rock.

They blew up in my face.

When he asked if I was okay I could only see his lips moving.

It took two and a half hours for my ears to work again.

* * *

His Dad took us out in their boat to ride on the tubes. They pulled two tubes at once.

It was a cloudy day. Raining off and on.

As soon as the wind started licking at our faces the battle began.

When our tubes came close I jumped off of mine knocking us both into the water. It strained our arms to climb back into our respective tubes.

Before we got back up to normal speed he jumped off his tube kicking me into the water, safely landing in my tube.

I floated in the cold water waiting for the boat to loop around to me.

I hoped it wouldn't storm.

Year V

He punched the cop in the face and got back into his car.

* * *

I skipped three stairs at a time. My arms full of shoes and socks
and a sweatshirt. I tried to hurdle over the small blockage used to

keep his dogs out of the basement.

My foot hit the top of the makeshift fence and I fell into the wall. There was a hole the size of a softball.

Our Friend with Glasses said, Oh man, his mom is going to be pissed.

He came out, still on the phone with his girlfriend. He rolled his eyes and went back into his room. He didn't seem to care.

I thought a ghost was behind me on the stairs.

* * *

He would sit next to me with red eyes while I read a book.

He told me later that he always thought I knew he was stoned.

I never actually did.

* * *

Our Friend with Glasses and he smoked cigarettes while we walked through the park.

We were all minors.

When we got back to the house Our Friend with Glasses' dad smelled the smoke and said he and I had to leave.

He smoked cigarettes while I drove him home.

He blew the smoke out the open window.

* * *

We both got cut from the baseball team.

* * *

We went to a rock concert. When the headlining band started playing he disappeared into the crowd.

Our Friend with Glasses and I stood off to the side watching the show.

Towards the end of the set the band's drummer started to play a face-melting solo. We were in awe.

As soon as the full band started playing again we noticed a familiar face float by.

He was surfing the crowd, yelling at us.

While he yelled we stared and watched him fly by.

* * *

We didn't want to play sports anymore.

We wanted to start a band.

* * *

His Dad rented a lake cabin. Only, it was a mile from the water.

He and I walked down once in four days.

The day we arrived His Dad sprinted up the stairs and took the bedroom on the upper level. That left him and me with one of the two bedrooms on the main floor. His sisters took the other one.

The main floor rooms had full beds, not big enough for two fifteen-year-old boys.

I spent every night watching television after everyone went to sleep.

On the last day he and I went upstairs to use the phone.

His Dad had been sleeping on a king-sized bed alone.

* * *

I wanted to try out for the talent show. Our Friend with Long Hair was going to play guitar. He was going to drum. I was going to sing.

I didn't have the voice for it.

* * *

We were at a church all-nighter.

Many of us sat outside waiting to go to the next destination. The downtown streets were deserted.

A Man in a Suit walked by.

"Do you have the time?" he asked.

The Man in a Suit looked at his watch and said, Twenty-two.

"Twenty to, or twenty-two what?"

Just twenty-two, the Man in a Suit replied.

There was silence.

The Man in a Suit began to walk away.

"What are you up to tonight?" he asked.

The Man in a Suit started to tell us about buses and bombs. Plants and planes.

Every time the Man in a Suit went to leave, he would ask another question.

* * *

I played drums for four years, improving little by little.

He decided to sit down at the set one day and was better than me.

I started playing guitar more.

* * *

My Mom let me stay the night at his house the day before the first day of school. I was surprised. She had never allowed this kind of thing before.

My Dad watched the football game with His Dad and then left.

We stayed up watching music videos.

The first day of school isn't ever important.

* * *

His Mom paid us to paint their barn.

We spent three days of summer climbing ladders and getting sunburned. But we finished.

Years later he told me that His Mom said it wasn't a very good job.

* * *

The van broke down in the fourth hour. It had to get towed to a nearby auto garage.

His Dad rented an SUV to finish the trip.

On our way back we stopped to get the van. His Dad made him drive it to the rental car drop off.

He was nervous he was going to get pulled over.

* * *

We wanted long hair if we were going to be in a real band.

We never had long hair before.

* * *

We would wander the hallways between classes.

We didn't like busywork.

But we did like spending time doing nothing.

* * *

"I got a bus boner today," he said.

"I hate that."

"I know. Every time you hit a bump it just gets harder. It seems like it will never go away."

"Sometimes you have to sit on the bus and wait for everyone to get off."

"Yeah," he said. "I just tried to hide it today."

* * *

I stayed the night at his house one weekend.

He kept me awake with his farts. I told him to stop too many times.

Finally I stood up and started getting my things together.

"Okay, I'll stop," he said, "sorry."

I laid back down on his floor and didn't hear another fart all night.

I didn't know someone could fart on command.

* * *

He started listening to bands that I didn't like that much.

* * *

He asked me to go on a family trip with him to South Dakota.

He sat in the front seat listening to a portable CD player while I sat three rows back with the luggage.

His two sisters sat between us.

There was a portable DVD player, but his youngest sister controlled it by watching the same horse movie two times a day.

I sat cramped for thirteen hours without uttering a word.

* * *

We would play H-O-R-S-E on the drums. He would always win. But for some reason the simpler beats were harder for him to play.

* * *

It was like a cuckoo's nest.

He told us his roommate was nice, but not complete behind the eyes.

When His Mom asked if Our Friend with Glasses and I wanted to visit him we said yes.

He wasn't how I expected. He was himself.

After he got out I never asked what caused the pain. I only knew he was in pain.

Year VI

He had a chaotic style of drumming.

* * *

He moved out of the neighborhood to the country.

I thought it would've been harder to hang out.

* * *

Our Friend with Glasses sang and played guitar.

Our Friend with Long Hair played guitar.

I played bass.

He played drums.

Our songs tended to speed up.

* * *

He told me he passed his driving exam with an eighty-two. The minimum to pass is an eighty.

The Test Man made a mistake when tallying up his points. Two had to be subtracted from the total. He passed with the minimum.

* * *

"Can I borrow this?" he asked, holding up a CD. I had gotten it two days prior.

"Sure."

When I got it back there was a hole burned into it.

"Sorry," he said. "I'll get you a new one."

"Don't worry about it," I said. It didn't make that much of a first impression on me, either.

* * *

Our Friend with Glasses drove to a girl's house. Our Friend with Glasses was trying to date this girl.

The rain shot down hard.

He and I jumped out of the white Buick and ran into the neighborhood. Our Friend with Glasses could find us later.

We took our T-shirts off so we could feel every drop sting.

* * *

The song we decided to play for the talent show was three minutes long.

He broke one of his drumsticks in the first fifteen seconds.

Our Friend with Glasses said a girl screamed in the crowd. The lights were too blinding for us to see anyone past the front row.

He played the whole song with one and a half drumsticks.

It sounded like he had a complete set.

* * *

"I tried liking her. I really did," he said.

"I don't care," I said.

My Life Long Friend had a crush on him.

My Life Long Friend was nice so he tried to reciprocate the feelings. He felt bad.

* * *

Our band played a competition that based its winners on majority votes.

We made it to the finals.

But lost by two votes.

It's a good thing. We would have eaten each other alive recording in Seattle.

* * *

His Dad took us to school so we could try out for the talent show. His drums were in the bed of the truck.

I climbed inside the vehicle in the middle of a silent fight.

His Dad's hand squeezed a water bottle.

There are two missing, His Dad said, did you take them?

He didn't respond. He continued watching the road move in front of us.

Answer me! His Dad slammed the bottle down, erupting the contents.

He never said.

But I bet he took them.

* * *

Our Friend with Glasses decided to start singing about Jesus and God. Our Friend with Glasses started telling people we were a Christian band.

He hated it when this would occur.

He didn't want the opportunity for more labels.

* * *

Our Friend with Glasses and he would stand outside the grocery store trying to get people to buy them cigarettes.

Sometimes people would call the cops and we would have to drive to a different store.

* * *

Time is relative.

* * *

He was walking his bike up a hill one day. An older friend asked if he wanted a ride.

He hid the bike in some bushes.

It was gone the next day when he went back for it.

* * *

We started playing more shows.

I think people started getting sick of the sound of our band name.

We made money from every gig.

Who would want to give that up?

* * *

He had a certain kind of routine.

—Walk into school with red eyes.

—Let his eyes clear throughout the day.

—Go to my house for band practice.

—Drink a glass of milk.

But before we started practice he would go to the bathroom to relieve himself.

One day was particularly stinky, so he borrowed my cologne and gave the room a few spritzes. The combination of smells gave

My Mom a migraine.

I wonder if he still had a routine after high school.

* * *

He didn't want to pack up his drums for our first show. He asked the opening band if he could use their drum set. The drummer said yes, but didn't look thrilled.

He was a hard hitter.

He broke the snare head and the bass drum pedal. It wasn't the highest quality set.

He packed his own set every time after that.

* * *

The Girl with the Lip Piercing asked us to pick one song that we would listen to for the rest of our lives.

"Ænema," I told her.

Our band broke up a year later.

* * *

"You know how difficult a task it is to flatter me."

* * *

Our Friend with Long Hair and I pulled into his driveway. When we got out of the car he came around the corner of the barn.

He was riding a horse, bareback.

* * *

The Owner of one of the venues we played at was set on making our city the next Seattle.

The Owner kept telling us we could be the next Nirvana with a little help.

We kept telling this guy to fuck off, silently.

The stage was like an oven. In the middle of the park it was the largest crowd we'd ever played for. There were a thousand people sitting on the grass.

Five minutes before we were to go on he wasn't where he was supposed to be.

Our Friend with Glasses and I stood behind the stage. We were getting nervous.

Two minutes before we were to go on he arrived.

Where the hell were you? we asked.

He told us our Manipulative Friend took him out to lunch. The Manipulative Friend knew how Our Friend with Glasses liked his girlfriend.

The stage was like an oven.

He took his jeans off and played in his boxers.

I don't think anyone noticed that he wasn't wearing pants.

* * *

It wasn't fun being in a band anymore.

Our Friend with Glasses, Friend with Long Hair, and I kept telling people that the band might break up.

He came up to us.

"I quit."

He never liked playing into the bullshit.

Year VII

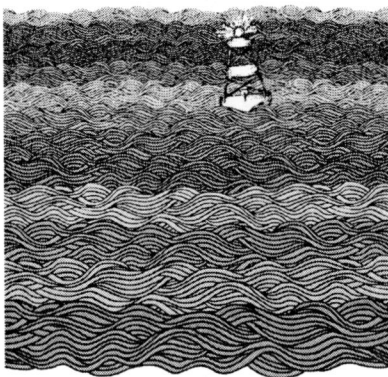

The world doesn't deserve him.

* * *

The light was green when he got hit.

The Other Driver was on the phone and had dropped something. The Other Driver's foot had come off the brake pedal for a few seconds.

It took only a second for his Blazer to get totaled.

The two of us watching the accident ran up to the three of them in his car.

The Girl with Dark Hair was hopping up and down, happy. The Girl with Dark Hair had always wanted to break an arm. His girlfriend was still in the car, having trouble breathing. Our Friend with Glasses told her, I love you. We never thought Our Friend with Glasses would actually say it out loud. What was more unexpected was when she said, I love you back. Nothing more ever happened between the two of them.

He was running away, down the center of the street. I took chase. It was eleven at night so I wasn't worried about him getting hit, but the ambulances were arriving.

I grabbed him and eased him to a stop.

"What are you doing?" I asked.

"Don't tell my mom about my car."

I wonder if the whiplash bothered him in his life.

* * *

His Mom said it wasn't a secret that he smoked pot. She told him that he was an adult and there was nothing she could do.

"You're just jealous," he told His Mom.

His Mom laughed, recalling this memory.

* * *

I stood in the back of the room for the acoustic talent show.

He walked up to the piano. He was nervous and didn't attempt to hide the fact.

He was three minutes into Beethoven's "Moonlight Sonata"

when he made a minor mistake.

Instead of continuing like nothing happened, he dropped his hands from the keys and said, "Fuck," loud enough for me to hear. His eyes scanned the crowd and I wondered what he was going to do.

He looked back at the sheet music and played the song from the beginning.

* * *

I went with him to his girlfriend's house.

Her mom was teaching everyone how to properly make macaroni and cheese.

"You're supposed to put butter in that?" I asked.

His girlfriend's mom laughed at me and said, Yes.

"Huh, I need to read directions more often."

I thought it was going to be a quick stop in. We ended up watching a two-hour movie and eating macaroni and cheese.

This was a great night.

* * *

He would quiver because of the medication he took.

It made it amusing to watch him eat.

* * *

He wanted to cover a Pixies song.

I would play guitar. He would sing.

I learned the song.

We never ended up playing it.

* * *

How many people actually find their identity in high school?

How many find it in college?

Or find it post-college?

Or ever?

* * *

We were driving home from downtown at midnight.

He came up fast on a red light. I yelled at him.

He slammed on the brakes, bringing his car to a stop in the middle of the intersection.

"Sorry," he said, backing his car up to the white line.

What was the point of backing up once he was halfway through?

* * *

He wouldn't answer his phone one night.

He wasn't where he said he was going to be.

He had disappeared.

Our Friend with Glasses, our Manipulative Friend, and I went into the city looking for him. But he wasn't in the city. We spent the night going from music show to art show hoping he was tucked away in some dark corner.

His Mom called me and told us they had gotten ahold of him.

He was driving across the state. His Mom told him to pull over in the next town and wait for them. He did so. He waited three and a half hours for them to arrive.

"Why did you pull over?"

"I don't know. My mom told me to."

"Why did you answer your phone?"

"I don't know. I got confused."

He was heading for Seattle. He was going to stay with a childhood friend. They had kept a connection.

He never told me why he was trying to run away.

* * *

He started reading about other religions.

I never found out how his parents felt about this.

I don't know what he settled on.

He would call himself an agnostic.

* * *

In art class, if he didn't like a painting he would wash it in white and start over.

Every assignment he turned in had seven layers.

* * *

The rain was spattering my windshield, I was stifling my desire to wipe it away.

"Why aren't you wiping?"

"This gives me a small difference in looking at the world. Makes life art. Almost impressionistic."

* * *

He popped the bumper off his car backing out of the driveway one day.

He was in a hurry so he shoved the bumper into his back seat.

Then continued on his way.

* * *

We sat around for two hours trying to figure out *Donnie Darko*.

We never came up with a solid explanation.

The next week we watched *Waking Life*.

* * *

He was not afraid to ask people what words meant. If someone said something he didn't understand, he'd stop the person and ask them to explain.

He had a better vocabulary than I did.

* * *

He called and asked if I wanted to go watch an author read at a local bookstore. I had never heard of the writer, but he said the man was good.

The place was packed.

That night made me want to read more.

Year VIII

We both decided it was the Mona Lisa.

* * *

He interrupted me while I was reading a book once.

"Does it count if you stick your dick in, change your mind, and pull it out?"

"Maybe?" I replied.

* * *

We tried writing a book together.

It was formatted like a popcorn exercise.

* * *

Ashes scattered the wake.

* * *

"Do you ever just want to punch something?"

He had cuts on his hand.

"Sometimes," I said. "Did you punch something?"

"No."

I didn't make the connection until I went to the bathroom in the east wing.

There were pieces of mirror in the sink and on the floor.

* * *

We sat around the fire. He rolled me a cigarette.

My Mom looked over at me, Are you going to start smoking?

"No," I replied.

* * *

We would play chess on Friday nights at a coffee shop.

It was as if we were old men.

* * *

He wanted to go out on a double date.

We were going to take the bus downtown and watch a local production of *The Wizard of Oz*.

My girlfriend and I sat at the Park & Ride waiting for him and his girlfriend to arrive.

He pulled up by himself.

I asked him where his girlfriend was. He shook his head. He didn't seem to be in a bad mood, so I didn't think they had been fighting.

"You guys can go ahead if you want, I don't want to make things uncomfortable."

"Not at all, come on," I said.

We took the bus and acted as if we were on a double date, minus one.

On the way home the bus hit a car while trying to make a right-hand turn. We sat on the bus waiting for forty-five minutes.

We had to take a different bus to get home.

* * *

"I have to be the first one you tell when you lose your virginity."

"Okay."

"No, you have to tell me first. Even if you have to call me at four in the morning. I want to be the first to know," he said.

"She'll know before you, I think."

"Promise me."

* * *

It was a school night. Around 10:00 p.m. we decided to go watch *The Life Aquatic*.

I don't remember deciding to do something so late on a school night before.

* * *

We pulled the car to the curb. The garage sale didn't look all that great, but we didn't have anything better to do.

It was as bad as we were expecting, but we found two disfigured objects that looked like trolls. They were fifty cents.

It was like having a friendship necklace. But for boys.

* * *

I bought a hat that I thought would work with long hair.

He bought the same hat a week later.

Only it was a different color.

* * *

I wanted him to like my girlfriend.

He said he did.

No one else seemed to get along with her.

I wondered if he was lying for my benefit.

* * *

If color is present because it is a reflection of light, would a green wall still be green when we turn the lights out? our Friend Who Can Sing asked.

"Yes," he responded.

But how? our Friend Who Can Sing asked.

"When you turn the lights back on, it'll still be green."

But how are you completely sure that it is green when you can't see it?

"If you leave a chair in the middle of the room, and turn the lights out, you can still walk into it."

An object is different than a color. When you turn the lights out the wall loses the quality of that color.

"And only in light does it reflect green?"

Yes.

"Then it has the potential of being green when the lights are out."

* * *

People didn't want to talk to me because I was shy around strangers. This trait of shyness made me come off as either rude or weird.

But people didn't mind talking to me when he was there.

* * *

He wasn't wearing a seatbelt.

* * *

A cut refused to heal on his forearm. It was deep. Day after day it didn't get better.

"What happened?"

"I was running through a parking lot and ran into a piece of wood sticking out of the back of a truck."

He told me years later that he sat in his room, sawing into his arm with a steak knife.

I've always been a gullible person.

* * *

He passed all three sections of the required state exam.

I passed one of the sections.

* * *

A friend gave me two coats that an ex-boyfriend left when they broke up.

The light-colored, leather and wool coat fit me. I kept it.

The dark-colored pea coat was small in the arms, but it fit him. I gave it to him. It fit him well.

* * *

We loved *The Sandlot*.

He searched the internet for PF Flyers.

He ended up finding them. But he didn't buy them because they were too expensive.

* * *

"Have you ever been desperate enough to masturbate to swimsuits?"

"No?"

* * *

All the girls had crushes on him.

Maybe it was his sense of not caring.

Or caring about the right things.

* * *

When did we grow up?

* * *

A friend's mom paid us to stain a fence. It was a big fence.

When he told His Mom we got this job she said, I hope you do a better job than you did with the barn.

He told me what His Mom had said. We didn't think the barn was a bad job.

We spent another week getting sunburned and stained. The stain was hard to push into the wood.

This time we did a better job.

* * *

It was the end of the year. My girlfriend was going to college in a different city.

I didn't see a future.

"How do you feel about it?"

"It happens. It probably wouldn't have worked out anyway."

* * *

I had him lie in a broken concrete cylinder. It was for a photography project. He was to look dead. Like from a war.

It was my favorite picture from that roll of film.

I've always been fascinated with death. In awe of the failure of life.

I had no idea.

Year IX

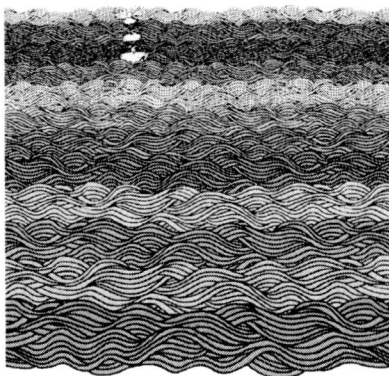

He played guitar with his thumbs.

* * *

The sound of a baby's laughter woke us up. He rubbed his eyes, trying to force them awake.

"That's the greatest sound you'll ever hear," I said.

"The baby?"

* * *

He shaved his chest and stomach. He didn't like having body hair.

I could never bring myself to do it.

* * *

We stood outside the admissions building smoking cigarettes. There was a ten-minute break before our next class.

A Man with a Shaved Head walked up to us, Hey man, you got an extra cigarette?

He pulled out his pack and handed the man one.

Thanks, the Man with a Shaved Head said, you saved me fifty cents.

"What?" I asked.

"You can buy individual cigarettes at the gas station for fifty cents," he told me.

"Weird."

"Yeah, if you ever get desperate enough, you can always scrounge together some change."

* * *

"You should move in. It would make the rent so cheap."

"I don't want to live in a party house," I told him.

"It's not going to be a party house."

* * *

There are different ways to grieve.

* * *

We sat in our Philosophy 101 class. Finals were two weeks away, but we were thinking about Plato at that moment.

He raised his hand with a question.

The Professor called him by my name.

We corrected The Professor.

Sorry, I get you guys mixed up, The Professor said.

We didn't think we looked alike.

* * *

I signed up for astronomy with Our Friend with Long Hair. Neither one of us wanted to buy the ninety-dollar book.

He had taken the course quarters before us.

I asked if he still had the book. He said that he would never get rid of it because he was so interested in the subject.

He let me borrow his astronomy book for class.

* * *

He took five shots of whiskey in a four-minute block. No chasers. Then he went to bed.

When he woke up hours later he was covered in blood and vomit. There was a hole in his window.

One of his roommates told him he tried to get up to puke, tripped on a shoe, punched a hole in his window, and passed out.

The cut in his arm was the only reminder of the incident.

* * *

The Blond-Haired Man and I tried to poop in a plastic bag. We were going to leave it in his bed.

Neither of us had to go to the bathroom.

We wrote a note to put in the bag instead.

When the Blond-Haired Man went to put the bag on his bed there were two people sleeping. The Blond-Haired Man had woken them up.

I wondered if they had sex, or just fooled around.

* * *

We drove past one another going opposite directions. I was leaving school, he was on his way.

My phone rang.

"Where are you going?"

"Getting a tattoo today."

"What about school?"

"Skipping."

"Fuck school, can I come?" he asked.

"Yeah."

He somehow managed to arrive at the shop before me.

* * *

He came out of the movie. I was watching the lobby from Customer Service.

"How was it?" I asked.

"Good. We should go tomorrow," he said, "I'd see it again. I'll call you."

He didn't call.

We didn't end up going.

* * *

I woke up to a scream.

My Brother's legs felt like rubber. My parents and I moved

My Brother to the floor. My Mom didn't wipe the vomit away from My Brother's mouth while trying to give mouth-to-mouth resuscitation.

It was a combination of methadone and crack cocaine.

My Brother was dead an hour before My Mom woke up to find her son.

He was the first person I called from the hospital.

* * *

"I like rolling my own cigarettes. You can have a small cigarette, or a big one. Cater to your needs."

* * *

We lay on our backs looking at the stars.

The stars mirrored themselves on the water's surface.

What would Rorschach see?

We didn't have to respond.

* * *

After three days we disconnected My Brother from life support.

I walked down the sidewalk not sure of where to go.

My Lifelong Friend followed me out. Was I okay?

Sometimes I don't understand that question.

I wanted to be alone.

He came over that night. He didn't ask if I was okay.

He didn't say anything.

He was just there.

* * *

He could talk to people more easily than I could, but he still always invited me along.

* * *

We arrived at the campground and drove around looking for the specific site. It was the first one we had passed.

An Officer with a Mustache skidded up after we unloaded the car.

The Officer with a Mustache demanded to know who owned the white car.

He stepped forward and asked why.

You need to slow down, son, the Officer with a Mustache yelled.

"I wasn't speeding."

The Officer with a Mustache's head shook, No, I just got a call, and they said a white car went screaming through here.

"So you weren't here?"

The Officer with a Mustache paused, then said, I got a call.

He interrupted the Officer with a Mustache, "So you weren't here? You didn't actually see me?"

The Officer with a Mustache's face turned red, Slow it down, son, I'm letting you off with a warning.

* * *

He wanted to get out of the rain.

* * *

Our Friend with Glasses, he, and I went to a diner the morning My Brother went to the hospital.

This was the last time the three of us would ever eat breakfast together.

I wish the circumstances had been better.

* * *

"Did you want some of this tobacco joint?"

"No, thanks."

"They don't really get you high," he said, "but I like them."

* * *

It rained all three days we were there. All we could do was sit around the fire and wish we were at home.

* * *

We talked about getting pi tattoos. Neither of us were math people, but the idea of something chaotic continuing forever was too appealing. Life continued, even with specific deaths.

"Come on," he said, "it'd be like twenty bucks for both of us. Just little ones on our finger."

"Most places have a minimum price. It's usually like fifty bucks per tattoo," I said.

* * *

"Have you ever listened to Elliott Smith?"

"No," I said.

"You should."

* * *

He had to call me because he didn't know where the ICU was at Holy Family Hospital. He had walked in the front doors. I told him to stay where he was and I would go to him.

I continued to stay composed until he walked up to me and hugged me before I could say anything.

I couldn't hold it in and cried into his embrace.

He hugged me harder than anyone ever had.

* * *

Our Friend from Tonga came back from a two-year journey.

The Blond-Haired Man called the Man with a Buddha Tattoo to see if the party house was available. Then the Blond-Haired Man called me and told me to meet there.

When our Friend from Tonga came into the living room he was sleeping. The Man with the Buddha Tattoo and I were excited and we shouted.

He came out of his room and hugged our Tongan Friend. He was sleepy.

"It's good to see you."

Then he went back to bed.

* * *

He used to deliver pizza in a bad neighborhood.

It was the dogs he hated most at night.

* * *

He had me shave his head. I left a rat tail without his knowing.

He called me the next morning.

"Fuck you," he said.

* * *

He always said he wanted to get drunk with me.

We never got the chance.

* * *

"I was watching *Boy Meets World* a few days ago, it was the episode where Cory and Topanga get married, and I almost damn near cried when Shawn made his speech at the end … because I believe it is the same speech every friend will one day eventually have to speak—'as life goes on'—you know. Maybe this is why I miss you, because I already know now that I will miss you more than I will have ever missed anyone, and this will happen in the not-too-distant future. I mean it's depressing, but it's life … and I honestly can say that we have a friendship that will never die. And I could never forget you. And that is what prevents me from shooting myself in the head."

* * *

We were going to try and start an advertising company.

I would do the art. He would make the connections.

I never followed through.

I wonder if he tried to do his half.

* * *

I didn't see him as much.

But when I did nothing was different.

We still had the same sense of humor.

Year X

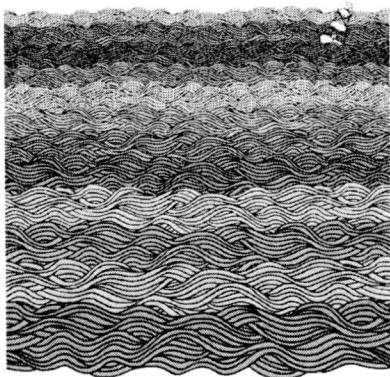

See a crack in the cement. Smell a certain scent. Hear a certain note. A certain style. Memories will come raining.

* * *

We bumped into each other on the first day of school. It was strange. New school, new campus, different schedules. I saw him eating an English muffin, sausage, and egg sandwich.

"Hey," I said, "how's it going?"

"It's fine. Funny bumping into you."

"I know, weird."

We looked around at the people passing.

"We should meet here every day. I have a break now, we should hang out."

"Yeah, definitely."

I never saw him at school again.

* * *

He never tried to pressure me into doing drugs.

* * *

Our Friend with Long Hair wanted to start a new band. I already said I would play bass. We wanted him to drum.

His set was missing a bass drum pedal. We couldn't start until he replaced it.

I went with him to get a new one.

* * *

He called me to see if he could come over and play a drinking game with us.

We were at my Friend with a Mohawk's parents' house. No one else was allowed over.

I didn't know what to say so I passed the phone to my Friend who Takes Pictures, who in turn, passed it to my Friend with a Mohawk.

He told me later that it was lame to pass the phone around the room.

"You could have just said no."

* * *

"Hey," I said.

He looked at me, taking a drag off his cigarette.

"First to know."

"What?"

"First to know." I walked back to the garage.

He called me that night.

"You son of a bitch! Nice job!"

* * *

He worked for the state for a while. His job was to babysit a grown man with mental instabilities.

"I watch TV for eight hours a day sometimes."

I was jealous.

Later he told me going to the grocery store with the man was
horrid.

He didn't like his job after the man attempted to attack him with
a steak knife.

* * *

He went to Italy for two weeks. His girlfriend lived there.

When he came back he said he felt out of place. He felt like he
belonged in Italy. All the time.

I wonder if that feeling ever went away.

* * *

I went to meet him at a fast-food restaurant.

When I got there he was leaning against his car.

"Hey, I already ate," he said. "Sorry, I was really hungry."

"Okay," I said.

"Did you want to get anything, or did you still want to hang out? Are you hungry?"

"I don't need to eat."

I don't remember where we went after that.

* * *

We stood on his back porch on a Friday night.

Music drifted out the open windows along with the fumes of a party.

We pulled American Spirits out of a rose bush.

"I'm glad we're still friends."

We tried playing structured songs. But he would change the drumbeat every few measures.

He woke up to screeching tires, sirens, and a crash.

He opened his front door and saw a car stalling in a fence. The Driver was fleeing on foot. He heard sirens, but didn't see the source.

He started chasing the man.

They jumped over a fence. The Driver was cornered.

The Driver pulled out a Phillips screwdriver, Fuck you, man, I'll stab you.

He was in an undershirt and boxers. Barefoot. "Fuck it," he thought and walked back home.

Some things just weren't worth it.

* * *

"I don't like rolling my own cigarettes. I've gotten into the habit of packing them too full, every time."

* * *

"Your brother has really affected me."

* * *

"I've tried meth, once."

"Yeah?"

He was over at our Grunge Friend's house when it happened.

Our Grunge Friend asked if he wanted to try it. He was always a guy to try something once. Our Grunge Friend's forehead had a meth boil in the center of it. A safety pin was sticking through it. Our Grunge Friend thought it would be funny.

"It made me feel so gross," he said. "If I ever do it again you have my permission to kill me."

He never did do it a second time.

* * *

He was going to drop out of school and backpack Europe for an undetermined amount of time.

* * *

He was trying to put in a new battery. He needed his car to get to work.

I tried handing him the battery across the engine, but we dropped it. It broke a little piece of plastic.

His radio didn't work after that.

I'm still standing by the fact that I didn't break his radio. It was just a piece of plastic.

* * *

We didn't hang out as much as we used to. But when we did, it was like there was no lapse in our lives.

* * *

I asked him to be in a video I was making.

He said yes, then asked what part he would be playing.

"A small one," I said, "but throughout the movie all the characters are looking for you. So through these conversations we learn who your character is. It's the most important part."

"Okay."

* * *

"Can I punch you in the arm?"

"Why?"

"Sometimes you just really need to punch something."

"Okay."

He hit me as hard as he could.

"If you ever need to hit me," he said, "just ask."

* * *

"There is a constant flow of feelings in a person's life, every second of his life. And all of them are too complex to even come close to putting down in words. Whoever said it is right, 'words do mean the least in what is actually being said.' If you find someone you can communicate well with on all aspects, which I think is a productive relationship, it is a meaningful one.

"What I'm trying to say is my goal for creativity is to transcend my feelings clearly to everything else. It's probably the same for every artist. And I think that doing so will get people to think and inspire them. To be more creative, more open-minded, and maybe people will actually start thinking for themselves once in a while."

He looked up at me. Then apologized. He said he was kind of stoned.

"On the other hand, you know how delicate human emotions are," he said, "how easily people can fuck with them."

That made me laugh.

* * *

He called me on the phone while I was at work. He was trying to kill time. I wasn't doing anything important either.

"Sorry I didn't make it up camping this year."

"Yeah, fucker, I was looking for you," I said.

"My mom said your girlfriend went with you."

"Yeah, she was there. I wanted you to meet her."

"My mom said that you guys seem pretty close. She said you seem to really like this girl."

"I do. I love her. That's why I wanted you to meet her."

"I want to."

She became my wife.

He never did get the chance to meet her.

* * *

We searched for an independently-owned diner to become regulars. We found some prospects. The problem was we couldn't stay consistent in attendance.

No one remembered us.

* * *

How far back can cause and effect go?

Year —

When he would need to prove his worth.

There is a time for peace and there is a time for action.

* * *

I missed his phone call.

In the message he said my name over and over again, not conveying any sort of message. I called him back.

"What are you doing tonight?" he asked.

"We're going to see a movie."

"Oh, so you probably don't want to hang out?"

"Probably not tonight."

"Okay," he said. "Are you guys hiring by chance?"

"Yeah, come on in tomorrow."

"Sweet, I'll see you then," he said. "We need to hang out soon. I haven't seen you in a while."

"I know," I replied. "We do, for sure."

* * *

He wasn't blackout drunk. But drunk enough.

It makes me wonder why the cop couldn't stop him. How the cop couldn't overpower a drunken man.

* * *

He was going to go to my place of employment and apply the next day.

* * *

He is more than a Memory.

* * *

The church always thought we were drug addicts.

* * *

I woke up to a phone call.

My Mom told me he died in a car accident the night before.

* * *

When did we grow up?

* * *

He punched the cop in the face and got back into his car.

He drove fast and hard.

Reason eludes us.

* * *

He missed the guardrail.

Would it have made a difference?

* * *

He took the ramp too fast at an awkward angle.

* * *

He wasn't wearing a seat belt.

Blunt force trauma to the chest.

They found him in the backseat.

* * *

My phone rang all day. People would ask me if he was okay.

"No," I said. "He's dead."

* * *

Our Friend with Glasses, my Roommate, Our Friend with Long Hair, and I covered "Let It Be" for the memorial service.

* * *

I read a eulogy.

I thought it was poorly written.

I wasn't in the state of mind to revise.

* * *

My Friend who Takes Pictures told me, His friends sat around his grave and drank beer on his birthday.

I wonder if they ever realized the irony of this action.

* * *

The flame burned a hole in the center of the eulogy.

My Friend who Takes Pictures asked if I was going to be okay.

"This would've been better if I didn't save it to my computer."

* * *

My Cousin walked up and hugged me.

My Cousin cried into the embrace. It reminds me of your brother.

I wanted to say it didn't remind me of my brother. It reminded me of him.

* * *

See a crack in the cement. Smell a certain scent. Hear a certain note. A certain style. Memories will come raining.

With each drop a vivid picture will pop into the head. A smile. A sob. A laugh. A moment.

I feel every drop sting.

* * *

I searched his room. His Mom had packed up all the stuff they had of his.

I emptied each box.

I couldn't find the troll.

* * *

There are different ways to grieve.

* * *

I'm having trouble breaking out of the narrow-minded way I was raised. Not to go back on everything I was taught, but to question and in turn reinforce.

I envy this quality that came so naturally to him.

* * *

He and I were supposed to take a cruise with our families a month after the accident. His family still went.

We had signed up to take a day trip with our dads months before.

The day trip never got canceled. But we didn't go.

* * *

His family sang "Silent Night." I saw him drift into one with the world.

* * *

Don't live in a world of "what-ifs." It will eat you alive.

* * *

His ashes were lost in the dark air. The wake behind the ship bubbled and foamed, but it didn't last long. I wanted to climb the railing and jump. I could have sunk into the waters and melded with his burnt self. I could have seen him again. Heard his laugh again. Felt that hug again.

* * *

"Wait for me," I said.

But he had already started swimming.

ACKNOWLEDGMENTS:

Thank you to Greg Gerding and the University of Hell Press—
what an honor to be among such a great body of work. I
appreciate the time and feedback from Ethan Wolcott, Meghan
Ayersman, Kelly Green, and Maureen Haeger. Thank you to
my parents, Ron and Karen, for a lifetime of support. Most
importantly, I am forever in debt to the Emery family for sharing
their son with the world.

ABOUT THE AUTHOR

Author Photograph by Kelly Green

Joseph Edwin Haeger has had work published in *RiverLit*, at *Zygote in My Coffee*, *Hippocampus Magazine*, and others. He lives in Spokane, Washington with his wife and son.

THIS BOOK IS ONE OF THE MANY AVAILABLE
FROM UNIVERSITY OF HELL PRESS. DO YOU
HAVE THEM ALL?

by Tyler Atwood
an electric sheep jumps to greener pasture

by John W Barrios
Here Comes the New Joy

by Eirean Bradley
the I in team
the little BIG book of Go Kill Yourself

by Calvero
someday i'm going to marry Katy Perry
i want love so great it makes Nicholas Sparks cream in his pants

by Leah Noble Davidson
Poetic Scientifica
Door

by Rory Douglas
The Most Fun You'll Have at a Cage Fight

by Brian S. Ellis
American Dust Revisited
Often Go Awry

by Greg Gerding
The Burning Album of Lame
Venue Voyeurisms: Bars of San Diego
Loser Makes Good: Selected Poems 1994
Piss Artist: Selected Poems 1995-1999
The Idiot Parade: Selected Poems 2000-2005

by Lauren Gilmore
Outdancing the Universe

by Robert Duncan Gray
Immaculate/The Rhododendron and Camellia Year Book (1966)

by Lindsey Kugler
HERE.

by Wryly T. McCutchen
My Ugly and Other Love Snarls

by Michael McLaughlin
Countless Cinemas

by Johnny No Bueno
We Were Warriors
Don't

by A.M. O'Malley
What to Expect When You're Expecting Something Else

by Stephen M. Park
High & Dry
The Grass is Greener

by Christine Rice
Swarm Theory

by Michael N. Thompson
A Murder of Crows
Days of Swine and Roses

by Sarah Xerta
Nothing to Do with Me

9 781938 753169